Bleeding Healing Heart Recall

Colette Cauli Brown

Copyright © 2021 Colette Cauli Brown

All rights reserved
ISBN: 9798744710323

The characters and events portrayed in this book are fictitious. Any similarity to real persons, living or dead, is coincidental and not intended by the author.

No part of this book may be reproduced, or stored in a retrieval system, or transmitted in any form or by any means, electronic, mechanical, photocopying, recording, or otherwise, without express written permission of the publisher.

Cover and print and ebook layout by: Cathy's Covers
www.cathyscovers.wix.com/books

Published by Colette Cauli Brown
colettejbrown@gmail.com

Editor: Ruth E. Walker
writescape.ca

Dedication

*Alistair James Brown – hubby, soulmate
May 8, 2014*

Introduction

As I write this introduction, I think about an upcoming anniversary: May 8, 2021, seven years since my hubby, best friend, and soul mate of 48 years passed away. Without James Alistair Brown, I feel lost on my Pilgrim Journey…but I hear his words of encouragement every step of the way.

In November 2019, upon my return from a Hawaii four-island trip with a group of widows, I end up having emergency open heart surgery to repair an abdominal aortic aneurysm ready to burst. My recovery was slow, my energy level was one hour per day. Having my fur Earth Angel buddies, Shep (a golden retriever) and Miss Daisy (a Morkie), by my side was my lifeline. I had to force myself to take them to my enclosed backyard, putting one foot in front of the other, and navigating stairs. Family and friends delivered homemade stews in crock pots to my front porch… feeding my body and my soul. I was in isolation four months before the pandemic started.

I would pick up a book for distraction. But because of lack of energy, concentration and poor memory, a great passion of mine was eroded from my reach. At Christmas, I received a gift of a book from my good friend Nancy Robichaud. The name of the book: For She Is the Tree of Life—Grandmothers through the Eyes of Women Writers, edited by Valerie Kack-Brice.

A book celebrating that connection with a collection of stories by authors. Wow, I love my relationship with both my grandmothers and love my relationship with my four grandchildren.

The best part? I could read one story at a time within this collection of stories and enjoy with the limited energy I had every day.

Thus, the concept for Bleeding, Healing Heart Recall was born looking at my own grief journey and the grief journey of others. I wanted the stories to reflect the healing recollection of both men and women. Being a clinical social worker for over 35 years, I knew the benefits of writing and drawing to help move through the trauma that life throws your way on your life journey. I invited persons of all ages and of different cultures to share their grief and healing journey. I promised confidentiality if they chose to use a nom de plume to share their story.

This is the invitation I shared.

Just a wee invite to share a life story sharing your Bleeding Healing Heart Recollection to be shared in my new book. My deadline is March 13th, 2021. You can choose to share anonymously or share your real name. You can share a poem, a journal entry, a chapter, a piece of art, a song, a melody, a quote, a photo. Your choice.

Your grief does not need to be resolved. You can have a bleeding heart now and be struggling now. Let me know yes or no in your reply. And I will send a reminder closest to my deadline. Thank you and remember I made an oath as a social worker of more than 35 years to keep what you share confidential.

Contributors are male and females between the ages of 7 to 89 years young. Every contribution is unique and is representative of a variety of healing life journeys. Hoping one word, one life shared, one piece of art and/or poem is able to help readers on their life Pilgrim Journ

Cradle Bleed

Lina - A knitted Hug
Lisa Petkovich – Not Alone
Colette Fortier – Intergenerational Grief
Colette Cauli Brown – Hoop's Life Story: Survival Leads to Love
Eve Victoria Hunter – Journal Entry
Arianna – Through the Eyes of a Child - Art

A Knitted Hug

Lina

I did not know half a century ago that she was about to become part of my story. We have never met you see, yet fate had chosen her to open her arms and her heart to my precious treasure.

I look back at my younger self and this is what I see. A sensitive 16-year-old girl, lacking direction, feeling unloved and searching for affection. She was sweet and not at all wise to the world. Mix an explosion of hormones with a handsome boy and her new reality unfolds!

It takes her to the city and with loving guidance from her sister and help from her mom, she awaits her admission to a home for unwed mothers. She is nurtured by the nuns and realizes that she feels safe there. She never wants to leave. But her time comes, just days after her 17th birthday. She is moved to the hospital to give birth to her precious baby.

After a few days, the social worker allows her to see and hold him but only once, and only for a few minutes. As she cradles him and looks into his eyes, she sees his need for love and recognizes the same need in herself! That fateful moment in time brings her to the realization that the kindest decision she can make is to give him the gift of a loving family.

The legal papers are signed and he's whisked out of sight.

Fast forward a half century later, an email message appears in my inbox from my sister. He's been searching for me through DNA records and found her on the web! He asked her to be a gatekeeper and to give me this message. "I am well and have had a life filled with love. I recognize the courage it must have taken to bring me into this world and let me go. I want to give my birth mom peace of mind. Please let her know that I love her."

When I read his words, I cry all of the tears that had been locked in my heart for so long! Though my husband has known from the beginning of our relationship, it was finally the right time to share that chapter of my life with our children.

With everyone's blessing, the conversation between our two families begins, evolving into much sharing of information and photos. How I loved hearing his voice for the very first time! Within six months, he travelled across the ocean to meet each of us in person.

As we gathered on the patio on a lovely sunny afternoon, he and his wife pulled up to the house. I walked slowly towards him and, the moment our eyes met, our souls remembered! There was no need for words as I hugged my son, now a grown man with a beautiful smile and a kind spirit. The time had come for our two families to blend into something new.

I have not yet had the opportunity to visit the mother who loved him and nurtured him but I've spoken to her. I hear the love in her voice and I feel her truth when she tells me that she has loved me from the day she first looked into his eyes!

Until we have the opportunity to meet, I have sent her a gift of a delicate lacy blue shawl. I knitted love into every stitch, and hope that when she wraps it around her shoulders, it feels like a warm hug between two moms.

Not Alone

Lisa Petkovich

The air has lifted,

Warm winds have shifted

Skies of blue and birds chirp songs

Welcoming you to your new home

Silent days, memories and calming rest

The wish and last remind

A suffering of a gentler kind

Hearts mend and prepare for what's next

This time of sorrow,

To respect, mourn and wait for tomorrow

Time encouraging the loving to go on

Remembering the soul is not alone.

Intergenerational Grief

Colette Fortier

"The Lord hath called me from the womb." Isaiah 49:1

In my senior years, while meditating, I received a message from my maternal grandmother Eleonore Frappier, from the Spirit World, that my mom loved me with all the love she had at the time of my birth.

I then realized that while my mom was carrying me in her womb, I absorbed her grief and her mother's grief. In 1944, my mom had to give up her career of choice teaching because in those years married ladies could not take away men's positions, let alone be pregnant and/or mothers could not work outside their homes.

Both my mom and myself were born in grief. My mom lost her fraternal twin in vitro. How horrible is that and she spent her whole life searching for him. My mom tried to find him in the foster son that she cared for and wanted to adopt while she was at home raising her four lovely daughters.

As a family, we all grieved the loss of a potential brother when he was returned to his birth mom. I found a new brother and friend, a maternal cousin Claude Mathe, the son of my mom's youngest sister. We were born three weeks apart. I will always be three weeks his senior and to this day we have an unbreakable bond!

Until a near-death experience, I received unconditional maternal love from my mom's other sister, my godmother, a VON nurse and mother of two older boys. I built a raft and attempted to cross the Mattagami River to visit my Godmother. I left without a floatation device and was found unconscious floating on the raft.

I was brought to the Timmins Hospital still unconscious, and my mom put the blame on her sister, my Godmother. I was solely responsible for this life-threatening event. And my mom barred her sister from my life. I was heartbroken and deeply hurt by my Godmother's perceived abandonment.

The day my Godmother left with her family from Northern Ontario to travel to the USA, I made a decision to not trust anyone but myself. I decided not to share my heart with anyone. I detached my heart from my family, from my friends and from my community, keeping my only link to my loving gentle dad and my cousin Claude, my friend and brother in arms.

As soon as I was old enough to leave home I wandered off with my only purpose to minister and care for the abandoned, abused children, youth and injured creatures I encountered on my life journey.

I remembered always, the native healing song my Grandmother taught me: "Mother Earth sing me a song, that will ease my pain, mend my broken bones, bring wholeness again. Catch my babies when they are born, sing my death song, teach me to mourn. Show me the medicine of the healing herbs. The value of Spirit, the way I can serve. Mother, heal my heart, so that I can see the gifts of yours that can live through me." Every day I cry lava tears "Hear my cry, Mother Earth...Help me heal this intergenerational grief buried deep in my heart."

Now, in my senior years, I realize I was the one who interfered with my mom's life goals and her career goals. It was not my fault but part of the history of my mom's era and I was not born a male.

Happy for me I lived in different times and was able to be both a mom and a career lady. I am in awe of my mom's journey. I now am able to receive her unconditional love. I now understand the grief she carried in vitro. I was called to this grief journey through her womb. I share my mom's grief, my maternal grandma's grief and now my own grief...as I now travel solo on my pilgrim journey.

Hoop's Life Story: Survival Leads to Love

Colette Cauli Brown

Hoop was conceived shortly after the Second World War, when his young mom fell in love with a medical officer 25 years her senior. At only one week old, Hoop was rushed to hospital with lung disease and spent the first year of his life attached to machines to help him breathe.

His mother, Peggy, fought many internal and familial demons – a sexually and physically abusive stepdad and an internal conflict with her own sexuality searching for the unconditional love of a father she never knew. She did her best to care for her son. Hiding his existence from her inner circle of friends, relatives and her abusive stepfather, Peggy travelled to a secluded region to raise her son.

After a few years, she realized that she needed to set her son free from the violence of her past life and allow him to grow up out of the shadows. She contacted the medical officer, Hoop's birth father and offered him the opportunity to raise his six-year-old son.

The conditions were set – Hoop would be raised by his dad and Peggy would forever give up contact with her son. They agreed that after the move, Hoop would be told that his mom had passed away so he would never attempt to find her. This agreement was sealed in blood drops, bleeding hearts from each parent.

Just before he left, Peggy promised Hoop that he could bring his favourite pony Duke to his dad's homestead – a family farm in Point Clark, on Lake Huron. So began Hoop's journey right into the arms of a sexual predator – the youngest brother of his birth father who, years earlier, lost his own son in a tragic car crash. Hoop's uncle used him as a slave – child labour from age six for most farm duties. He often raped Hoop in the barn by the cows, away from the rest of the family. During the violence he would scream obscenities and always end with, "Why did you not die in the car crash instead of my beloved son?"

Hoop learned at an early age to detach himself from the horror and travel to a safe place in his mind – his own loving animal kingdom. There, he searched for his long-lost pony Duke, who never did follow him as promised. Hoop developed his own communication with all the species; hence, he got his name Hoop the Animal Whisperer.

When Hoop was old enough to escape, he hitched a ride hiding in a truck under some stacks of hay. When the driver arrived home and got out to open his barn doors, Hoop snuck out and hid under a willow tree, concealed in its canopy of weeping branches until dark.

Hoop then walked in the dark on the side of the road for miles. At sunrise, he hid in the forest and slept during the day. He continued this travel by night on foot for a few days until he spotted train tracks and decided to see where they would lead him. The train system became his refuge.

During the day, Hoop rode in empty wooden train cars along the train route, used the train station washrooms, drank their water and ate from the garbage bins sifting through the half-eaten scraps from passengers, truckers, and railway workers. No one questioned him as he was picking up garbage and placing it in discarded containers for later, using a sock tucked in his pocket. He slept by day and travelled by night, often hiding in the parked train cars.

Some days he would be rudely awakened by the jerking back and forth when the train car was hooked to a moving train, and off he would go to a new destination.

He was not worried that his abuser would try to track him down. His uncle was getting a monthly income from his deceased brother – money meant to support Hoop until he reached the age of majority.

During his travels, Hoop was able to use his scuba diving training learned on the shores of Lake Huron and financed by his father. He viewed proficiency in the water as a survival skill in case he had to flee his abusive uncle or an oncoming train while walking on train tracks over a bridge.

Hoop also assisted the engineer on the Ontario Northland Train when a passenger passed out while travelling. A scream and a sharp whistle alerted Hoop someone was in distress. "Anyone know CPR?" Hoop quickly responded. "Yes, I am a trained first responder." He brought the middle-aged gentleman back to life… earning some spare change giving CPR. He had always wanted to follow in his father's footsteps who worked as a doctor and a pharmacist, but his dad had passed away when Hoop was in his teens but not before he secured some financial assistance for Hoop. This allowed him to receive basic medical training at Kitchener Waterloo Hospital.

In 1966, Hoop got off the train in Timmins. By then, he was accustomed to taking on odd jobs as they became available. As luck would have it, he was hired to work in the McIntyre Mines on a contract to scuba dive in the mines' deep waters and bring back rock samples to be tested for the presence of gold. Hoop's survival efforts paid off as the mines paid a hefty sum for him risking his life diving in the submerged mines.

A couple years later, Hoop met the love of his life and together they took the ONR train to Southern Ontario to start their new life together. This time Hoop rode coach like any other paying passenger. And while he was never reunited with his beloved pony, Hoop named his first dog, a St Bernard, Duke in its memory.

Journal Entry

Eve Victoria Hunter

*This is for the children,
whom I love and cherish,
and this is for me, Eve Victoria
and the scared, frantic child of
sexual, physical, emotional and spiritual abuse.
I love you. This is for you.*

Let words be the jewels on your necklace so costly and precious. Let sounds of birds chirping and gentle breezes through white sheer curtains be soothing to your soul. Can you smell the soft new tender dandelions growing in the fields all around you? They grow for you, they celebrate you. They shine in their bright sunny suits just for you. Jesus planted them here for you.

You can put on your white dresses here; the German Shepherds are keeping a watchful eye. You can run here. You can jump. You can laugh and you can sing songs here. Songs are good here. Made up songs, strung together words of freedom's sound.

You can play here. Go ahead and be free to get in the dirt. It feels so good on your toes. This is what freedom feels like, the earth soft and fragrant rushing through my fingers. Let's play. Let's make mud pies large and small. Pat them in full and tight to share with friends in ribboned pigtails and dresses. "I love you" one says. "I love you so much" says the other.

There is no fear here. This is where little girls come to play in peace. Angels are seen here. They tend to the gardens and play skipping with us. They are our friends. We love them and they love us.

The bad men are prohibited from entering this place. No ugly smell here, no awful taste in my mouth. You stink. You gross piece of scum. Ugly scum. No respect. I hate your breath and your very existence. You make US SICK. WE HATE YOU!

UNBELIEVABLE HATRED. Stealer of dreams. You thief. Ugly thief. Does your family know how ugly you are? Ugly suit and tie and dress shoes, hair slicked back. You reek of stink. You are rotten. You are *"Fuil. Goed"* (disgusting stuff) in Afrikaans.)

Guess what? I'm telling on you! Breaking News… A man in a Suit on the Pulpit uses and abuses little girls. We are telling, we are telling, *na-na-na-na-na*! What do you think now? They knew because of the stink. They knew that stink. Sex with children. Blood and semen! They KNOW NOW! We are NOT AFRAID OF YOU! You, however, be afraid of US, Child fucker.

The angels at the park brought me back my Voice. You had it in a safe with the others. But the Champion fought you and released the voices. And guess what? Be afraid because I'm telling my kids on you. I'm telling the world on you. Your tower has fallen. London bridges is falling down, falling down. My voice is a trumpet loud and strong. It echoes through the ages back and forth – releasing the Captives.

I am singing my inner child a song…. "You are my sunshine… my only sunshine."
I will record my voice and replay as often as any child of this world needs to hear the voice, the words, the melody and me leading them to freedom forever.

Sad Heart Fix

This is how Arianna looks when she is Sad. The Sun, her puppy and Daisy bring Joy.

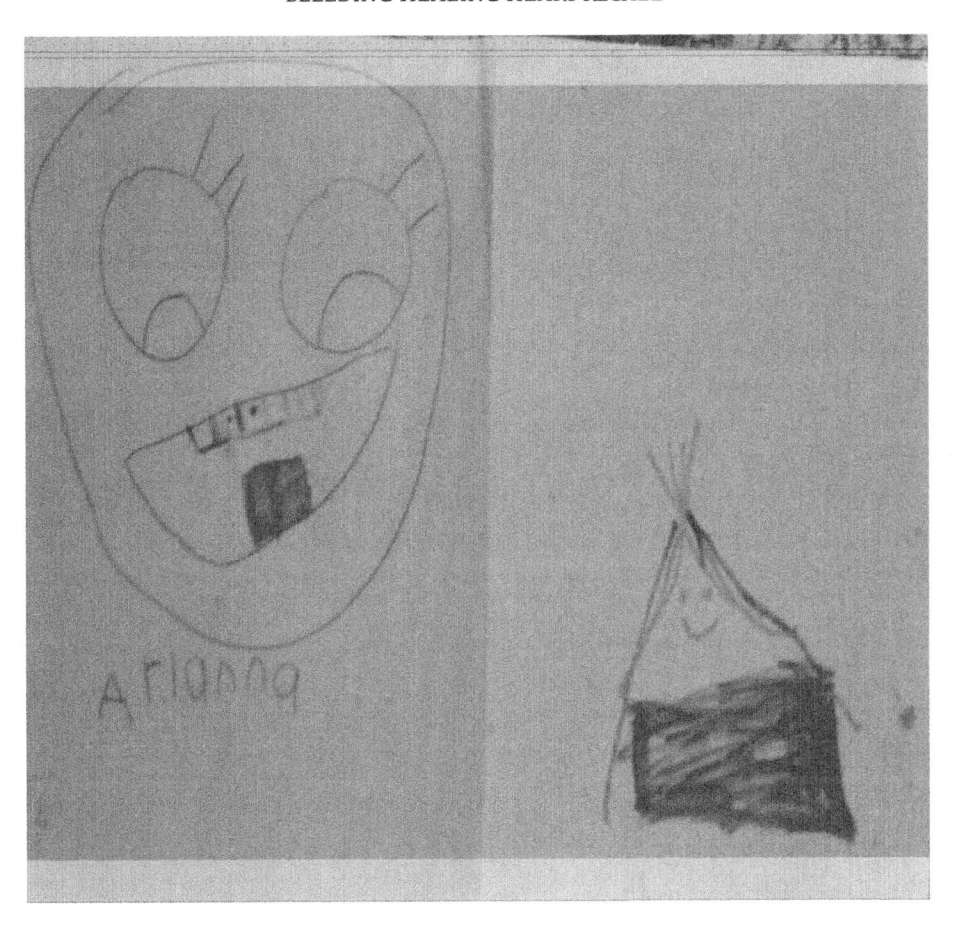

This is how Arianna looks when Happy. A comfy warm blanket in her tent brings Joy.

Hammock Heal

Nadine Cedars – Our Broken Family
Alivia Lusk – Tell All of Them
Art – Abby Lusk
Emma Lusk – Hurtful Words at Dinner
Darby Brown – Who Am I?
Colette Cauli Brown – Ode to My Dad
Colette Cauli Brown – For the Love of Shep Brown

Our Broken Family

Nadine Cedars

We were a typical family. Life was normal for myself, my husband, our son and daughters until a terrible tragedy changed everything. A pedophile damaged the childhoods of at least 23 young boys, and ruined many lives. Our son, aged 13 years young, was one of those victims.

The pedophile, his schoolfriend's stepdad, lived in a cabin accessible only by train once a day. There was no escape for those vulnerable and innocent boys who were also threatened with harm to themselves and their families if they ever told anyone.

In the aftermath of the abuse, we carried on with our busy lives not realizing why our son had started to change. He wanted to sleep with us saying he was having nightmares and kept repeating the number ten. When he wanted everything in his room to be black, we thought perhaps it was a fad of some kind — so we went along, wallpapering and buying black curtains and bedding.

Next came the phone calls from his teacher about his school absences, not handing in homework and failing grades. That is when the teacher recommended counselling. Our son got himself a paper route. But he was spending most of the collection money at the arcade and buying cigarettes. How he managed to graduate from grade school was beyond our understanding!

We couldn't have known that this was just the beginning. A few years later would come the street drugs and alcohol.

One day, out of the blue, our son asked if we had received a call from the Christian talk show 100 Huntley Street. Another red flag that we missed. Finally, after an assessment from a psychiatrist, the truth of the child sexual abuse was revealed to us.

The pedophile was charged and our son was asked to make a statement for court. His teacher happened to have been on the jury that convicted the man to six months in jail.

Even after seeing some justice, our son refused to go back to high school and it seemed that no one could help him move forward. He was trapped in a victim's web. The use of drugs and alcohol intensified as he started to hang around an older crowd.

After much deliberation, we made the difficult decision to send him to live with his bachelor uncle. He was a Big Brother which we hoped might equip him to support our son. A few years passed and his uncle helped him find a job. Soon after, our son met a divorced lady with teenagers and moved in with her. It was a troubled relationship as she also had suffered from addictions — for her it was pain medication and occasional gambling. Some of her family members did not like our son.

The relationship didn't last and before long he needed our help. He was laid off at work but after a while managed to find another temporary job. We co-signed a loan to purchase him a vehicle. Life went on.

Then, one day he was arrested and charged with selling drugs. We paid his bail and he was released into our care.

Through the years, he has been in and out of jail, had many failed attempts at different jobs, moved in and out with us, lived on welfare and lost his driver's licence. Recently, he was finally granted disability support due to his physical and mental health limitations, mainly COPD and PTSD.

We are in our 70s. Our stress level is unbelievable and has taken a toll on our health. My husband suffered a heart attack several years ago and I have many stomach issues and am trying to control my own alcohol use.

We are his last hope. Unfortunately, living with us in a fairly remote area has its drawbacks — the lack of help for victims of abuse. Every week or so, our adult son consumes large amounts of alcohol and/or cannabis. We go through the following five stages over a period of several days.

> Stage 1 - Talking out loud to himself all day and night long.
> Stage 2 – Looking for hugs and wanting confirmation of our caring.
> Stage 3 – Loudness, looking for attention, whistling and talking loudly.
> Stage 4 – The anger sets in, blaming, chastising and paranoia.
> Stage 5 – Retreating back into himself.

The stress is slowly killing all of us. It is just a matter of time. We are a broken family because of what this pedophile, this adult bully and criminal, did to our child. How do we heal from this trauma?

Tell All of Them

Alivia Lusk

Whether it's people
Whether it's pain.
Take that big leap,
That big leap of faith.

To love you first,
To love you first
Follow the Lord
And He will guide you.

Through all the pain
That really hurt you.
To love you first,
Just love you first.

Tell all of them
What hurt you
Tell all of them
What they put you through.

Tell all of them
How you feel
To put the past behind
And seal the deal.

To love you first
Tell all of them
How you feel
And seal the deal.

Art created by Abby Lusk

Hurtful Words at Dinner Time

Emma Eileen Lusk

I look at my own cracked, itchy and bleeding hands as they discuss someone else's
obsessive hand washing. This is a topic I can relate to very much. Their harmful,
judging words cut through me like a knife as my stomach twists into knots. I have
officially lost my appetite. I politely excuse myself to wash my hands yet again,
their words still playing over in my head like a never-ending song.

I dream of acceptance in our world that tries desperately to push out the different
and the messy. What they don't realize is that different and messy can be good.
It's a part of life. What may look like a fault in one's eyes looks like beauty in
another's.

Conquer those negative thoughts. Help others see how obsessive compulsive
disorder (OCD) does not hinder your natural beauty; it only adds to it!!

Who Am I?

Darby Brown (written September 9, 2014)

I was born June 5, 2000, at Markham Stouffville Hospital into the welcoming hands of a midwife. The date of my birthday makes me a Gemini. I have lived in Stouffville nearly all my life. I have an older brother Ethan who is in grade eleven and loves to play video games. My mother is a nurse manager and my father is a computer consultant and author. My grandmother lives in an apartment in our home with her animals. My grandfather was also living with us until May 8, 2014, when he died.

We also have two dogs, one named Lexie and the other Samantha. As a family, we enjoy skiing in the winter, walking the dogs, swimming in our pool and watching movies together.

I have always been different but for most of my childhood I just never understood why. I finally learned why when my family decided to get me assessed. I used to think that I was "stupid" but after I went through all the assessments, they diagnosed me with ADHD Attention Deficit Hyperactivity Disorder. The assessments showed that my ability to retain short-term memory was very low. Thankfully, with a little medication, I was able to focus and retain knowledge.

At first, I was really scared that my peers' opinion of me would change or that they would even bully me, but all my friends were really great. Since being assessed and getting support, my marks in school have risen significantly and I have been less hyper in my everyday life. This has probably been one of the best things to happen to me, and I am so grateful to have had my family encouraging me along the way.

From the age of two, I put my heart and soul into dancing. I was a competitive dancer for most of my childhood. Even though I loved dancing with all my heart, at the age of twelve I decided to quit. The hardest part was leaving my friends that I had been with for almost ten years. It remains the biggest decision I ever had to make. At first, I thought it was a bad decision but now I know it was absolutely right. Since quitting dance, I have been doing competitive All-Star Cheerleading. Dancing from a young age gave me an advantage over others in the squad. Through cheerleading, I have made so many strong friendships and learned the importance of being on a team. We also won nationals two years consecutively and I am hoping we win again. It is really hard to go to competitions after winning nationals because everyone wants to beat you and prove that they are better than the past national winners.

To this day, I am still very happy with my decision to quit dancing and join cheerleading. Another activity I love is high jumping. Ever since I started track and field in grade four, I have loved high jump. I went to regionals and placed third. In grade seven, I jumped higher than the grade eight boys, and in grade eight I went again to regionals and placed fifth. I really hope to join the track and field team this year and do some more high jumping.

I have one career goal and one goal only, and that is to become a coroner. After high school, I hope to go to university and study to pursue my dream job. Most young people don't even know what a coroner is or why I dream of becoming one. A coroner is a doctor who investigates cadavers when a person has died of an unknown or unnatural cause. This is the job of my dreams because I find it very interesting — different than other careers. I find myself interested and fascinated in discovering how and why people have died.

I have not been through many life-changing experiences. The biggest and most recent was when my grandfather passed away from pancreatic cancer. It was really hard for me because I was so close to my grandpa and saw him every day. He played a big role in my life and taught me so many things that I will never forget.

Before my grandpa died, he and my grandma ran an animal rescue. Ever since I can remember, we have had animals. Not just dogs and cats but animals most people do not ever have. For example, we had a scorpion, an iguana, piranhas, tortoises, a large parrot, snakes and so much more. It was really hard having an animal rescue because most, if not all, the animals were injured and so many die prematurely. I love all animals and am so privileged to have as many as I do and be able to have tropical animals that most people do not have.

All the things I have gone through have impacted my life and have made me the person I am today.

Ode to my Dad

Colette Cauli Brown

Northern Cobalt welcomed your birth.
Middle lost child, in search of Joy.
Shared memories, river logging.
Gentle presence, infectious smile.
Best man at your cousin's wedding
Leads you to Mom, Timmins romance.
Plumber by trade, golfer's man cave.
A peace maker, yearly Blessings.
Guiding parent, storyteller
Calm and loving, gentle spirit.
On Father's Day in Heaven, Dad.
Shared life's secrets on birch tree bark
Soft written words – Live life fully…
Whispered goodbye during my youth!
A phone trauma, a bleeding heart.
My beacon now, through life's journey.
Father's Day ode, healing my heart.
Forever more, soft gentle Dad.
Eldest daughter of four smart girls
Look up to you, my loving Dad
Sensitive heart, gentle aura.
Healing my heart forever more!

For the Love of Shep Brown

Colette Cauli Brown

2009 – 2020 Paw print on our Land

Earth Angel Shep
Senior Golden
Left a Furever
Paw Print
And Angel Hair
In our Hearts.
For the Love of Shep
Summer of 2020…Running Free…Forever more.

So this is where we part Sheppie
And you'll run on, around the bend.
Gone from sight, but not from mind,
The angel fur I stroke and kissed
Your place I'll hold within my heart
You'll be so missed forever more….
Dreaming of your gentle spirit…

Shep chose me, our eyes connected
Brought you home for Jack to train you
When Jim passed you chose to serve me
Six years you walked my grief journey
Through my fog you lit my dark path
Walking steps behind the moss trails
At Thistledown, Heaven on Earth.

Survived life-threatening surgery
With you by my side my Sheppie

January 2020...
You face slow gradual blindness
Sharing our worst fear you and me...
Laser healing for me alas
Losing your way on the moss trails!

So this is where we part Sheppie
Now you are free to roam with Jim
In the Heaven's above furever.
A Red Fox Lab, Benson, found you
On Crown Land tucked under a tree.
Scattered bones ripped collar ID
Peace of mind till we meet again.

Special thanks from deep in my heart to the best team grief counsellors: Nancy and Colin Graham - Owner of Thistledown Pet Memorial, Uxbridge, where Shep took a turn around the bend and got lost in the Durham Forest adjacent to our favourite trails at Thistledown - my little piece of Heaven on Earth!

A shout out to:
Team Chelsea, and their many volunteers who tirelessly searched for my Golden Retriever in their safe bubble from August 1, 2020 'til the day Shep's remains were found in Durham Forest.

And to Stephanie & Keith Russell, and their puppies Benson and Jedi, who found the remains of Shep, his ripped collar and ID during their walk in the Durham Forest November 14, 2020 giving our family Peace of Mind. They returned and marked the spot with a cross and a stuffed toy to help our family and friends through our grief.

Spinning Wheel

William Morgan – A Spiritual Awakening
Colette Fortier – Coeur d'Amour
Chelsea Mack – Heart of Love (Coeur d'Amour translated)
Scott Rose – Life Adventures
Amber Houle – Colour Healing – Art
Beth Bowman – Continuing to Leap for Joy
Valentina Gal – Jim Brown Our Unsung Sport Hero

A Spiritual Awakening

William Morgan

In 1985, as a young man, I was thrilled to be starting my career in social work. It meant moving from my hometown in southern Ontario to the largest city in Canada. I started as a youth worker at a halfway house in Parkdale, a low-income area in Toronto's west end. This experience opened my heart to human suffering and led to a discovery of my true self. I met many wonderful people there and learned more from the residents than they learned from me.

Later that year, I made the important decision to accept a position with a large bureaucratic Catholic non-profit in the area of child welfare. I was sad to be leaving the halfway house so soon, but I looked forward to this new opportunity. I was idealistic and totally naïve to the realities of office politics.

As a novice child welfare worker, I was not prepared for the demands that such a position required of me. When my supervisor described the serious cases to me, I felt so much anxiety that I started laughing. I respected him because of his honesty and supportive attitude about my learning. My confidence grew significantly along with my feelings of joy in this new position. I went from a very quiet, meek person to a more assertive and expressive individual. I was absolutely thrilled with this transformation. I was meeting more people than I had met in my entire life and developing new skills especially intuition and compassion.

After three months, my supervisor was demoted to another office. Instinctual fear permeated my entire being. I felt very alone, isolated in a new challenging career and lost in a very big city. During this time, I went from great joy and happiness to acute fear and shock. My sense of security and stability pulled away from me; I experienced a complete loss of control. With organizational politics beginning to play out, I entered fight or flight mode. The fear (insecurity) within me began to manifest itself as anger and aggression toward my new supervisor and office manager.

I needed so desperately for someone to come into my life and protect me. I wanted to feel the loving presence of God.

The Catholic social work organization was revealing its shadow, in complete opposition to values I had learned in both social work and through my Catholic education. I felt like I was in the middle of a dream or more like a nightmare but it was real. I struggled for months with my supervisors, knowing deep down that I was in a losing battle since they held all the power.

Days before Christmas, my employment in child welfare was terminated. It was just before my six-month probation period ended.

This traumatic loss for me was so cruel and painful that it felt like a death. I began to lose my lifelong faith in a personal loving God. I went through a long grieving process involving anger and sadness. It was very challenging living all alone in a large city. Given my lack of a graduate degree in social work, I struggled to find another job in the same field. This despite seven years of university education in a liberal arts, social science degree as well as undergraduate social work training.

Not only was I feeling profound grief, but I was experiencing a deep feeling of rejection. My inner life went from great joy and compassion into the darkest of depressions. What I did not realize at that time was that the Holy Spirit was very close to me, aware of all my frustrations and emotional suffering.

Many special people entered my life at this time, I believe that they were holy angels (messengers of the light). One was a beautiful woman, a colleague of mine from the child welfare agency who contacted me a few months after I lost my job there. I always knew that she carried within her a very powerful healing spirit filled with loving-kindness and compassion. She told me about a promising clinical social work position in the city of Oshawa which led to my employment there in fall 1986.

I was so happy to be working at a small child and family service agency, under the supervision of a social worker and Catholic nun. In my new position I learned art and play therapy with children and relational family systems treatment — which were so helpful to so many clients. I could feel the strong presence of God within and outside me. The presence of a Catholic Church nearby added to my feelings of the power of the Holy Spirit.

Since I was still feeling sad and betrayed by my previous employer, my supervisor recommended that I meet a holy man in the downtown area — a blind spiritual healer (mystic). I called the mystic and he spoke to me about going on a journey, an inner one. With these words, I sensed a great peace from his voice.

I met with him in a very small chapel, it was a hidden treasure located in a very busy downtown section of the city. At my first visit to the spiritual healer, it felt like I was meeting Jesus Christ himself.

In his presence, I felt a loving, humble and peaceful spirit beyond anything that I had ever encountered. This spiritual healer combined contemplative prayer from the Holy Scriptures (in braille) with highly in-depth Jungian psychotherapy.

The greatest lesson that I learned during this time came from St Paul: "it is in weakness (gentle compassion) that we find strength." This concept is not accepted in the secular world. The profound healing and spiritual transformation from this holy man dramatically changed my entire life. I have never forgotten him and know that he is a saint in modern times.

In 1987, while practicing solitary meditation, I envisioned a monk in a brown robe sitting at an old table with a lit candle and a holy book. In a moment of synchronicity, I was invited to a silent retreat by the Knights of Columbus at the St. Augustine monastery in northwest Toronto. These sacred memories have never left my consciousness. I learned about the mysterious nature of a religious calling and the divine presence in monastic life.

Thirty-five years later, these powerful memories have never left me and I now realize that I experienced an awakening in my spiritual life journey. The Holy Spirit guided my soul through cruelty, disillusionment and pain, and introduced me to the discovery of sacred truths involving forgiveness, healing and eternal love. In 1985, my symbolic death at the large child welfare agency, created inner conditions for a transformation into my true authentic self, in alignment with the Universe.

In loving memory of my holy friend, Mario
Galeazzi, St. Stephen's Chapel.
"Life is not a problem to be solved, life is a mystery to be lived"

Coeur d'Amour (Heart of Love)

Colette Fortier

Se recueillir pour l'accueillir
L'amour qui represente l'attente,
Blotti, sous l'ecorce apparente
De l'etre humain tout en desir!
Dans le silence de la foi
Se cherche le jet de confiance
Qui se refait, a la nuance
Un Coeur d'Amour en soif de vie
Presence douce et attentive
A cette presence qui eclate
Come le coeur d'une marguerite
En feuilles de neige sur la rive
Se recueillir pour l'accueillir,
Jour apres jour tu dois subir
L'eternel routine se repete
Comme le movement
D'une mer qui fuit
Enleve le masque de la vie
Et tu frisonnes
L'hypocrite ideal
De notre douce enfance

Il faut reflechir pour voir
Que dire de l'experience
Neuve, folle, frivolite
De l'enfance possible
Que tu revis en reves
Tu as perdu ta jeunesse
Folle, douce memoire
Du veillard qui se meurt
Deforme ton coeur d'amour
Ta vie n'est que desir
Tu domines en silence
Cette discipline me forme
Tout en etouffant mon esprit
Mais enfin tu es libre
Se recueillir pour l'accueillir
Tu communies l'ivresse
Du verre de la bouteille
Tu jouis du monde irreel
Un jour de l'enfance
Qui se meurt a petit feu
Parce qu'il faut veillir
Pour t'adapter a la citee
Que dire de la noire existence
De l'etre humain sans espoir
Qui trotte seul confus
Comme l'aile de l'horloge antique
Maudite qui tourne en rond

Se recueillir pour l'accueillir
Folle vie de l'homme sans Dieu
Ca libere de se creer un Dieu
Aussi humain que possible
Pour etre enfin compris!
A quoi bon vivre s'il faut mourir
Sans atteindre l'equilibre
D'un coeur claire comme le soleil
L'amour qui brille dans la nuit!
L'amour qui repose en attente
De notre douce enfance!
Se recueillir pour l'accueillir
Mais enfin tu es libre!
Coeur d'amour coeur de guerison.

Heart of Love (Coeur d'Amour)

Translated by Chelsea Mack

To collect ourselves to receive them
Love that represents patience
Blossoms under the visible bark.
A desirable human being
In the silence of faith
Looking for the jet of confidence
Which is redone in the shade.
A heart of love, strong with life
With a soft and attentive presence
To this exploding presence
Like the heart of a daisy
In sheets of snow on the shore
To collect ourselves to receive them
Day after day you suffer
The eternal routine repeats itself
Like the movement
Of an escaping ocean!
Removing the mask of life
And you shiver
The ideal hypocrite
Of our soft childhood
Think to see
What can we say of the experience

New and crazy
Of possible childhood
That you live through dreams
You lost your childhood
That you live through dreams
You lost your childhood
Crazy, soft memory
Of the dying old man
Deforms your heart of love
Your life is only desire
You dominate in silence
The discipline reforms me
All while chocking my spirit
Finally you are free
To collect ourselves to receive them.
You share drunkenness
Glass from the bottle.
You enjoy the made up world
A childhood day
That is slowly dying
Because we need to wake up
To adapt you to the city.
What can we say of the dark existence
Of the human being without faith
That walks around confused
Like the wing of the antique clock
That keeps turning in a circle
To collect ourselves to receive them
Crazy life of man without god!
To create a God

As human as possible
To finally be understood.
What's the point of living if you have to die
Without reaching equality?
With a heart as clear as the sun
Love that shines at night
Love that rests while waiting
From our soft childhood
To collect ourselves to receive them
Finally you are free!
Heart of love, heart of healing!

Life Adventures

Scott Rose

As a kid, I developed a painful disability. I spent half my childhood in the hospital, looking for cures, or trying to be put on the right medications. As a senior I have had a whole lifetime to learn how to deal with this pain.

I have been to every hospital in Ontario – from Toronto to London to Oshawa. With having a disability, I had to learn how to make my own fun at home as my parents didn't allow me to play with the other kids. Unsurprisingly, my social skills dropped to zero as I grew up basically a loner. Mom and Dad tried to make sure that I had everything and even installed a pool in the backyard. That is where I taught myself how to swim with a lifejacket on.

In my twenties, I moved out and got a 995-square-foot condo. It was a real time of independence and growth. I attended the opera and ballet, swam at an outdoor pool, went to events and travelled by myself.

On my 25th birthday I was on board the S.S. Carnival when my cabinmate shared the word of God with me. A couple of words that got my attention was Jesus will be your friend and be there when you need Him. On the 27th of August, I accepted Christ as my Lord, changing my life forever. I thought that being a Christian was going to be easy, but it was harder than my life before. The familiar poem "Footprints in the Sand" when Jesus walks along unseen, sticks with me through troubled times.

As a Christian, my walk with God felt strong but many people told me that I would never know God to the fullest until I hit rock bottom. The year 2019 was my rock bottom. I can remember one day feeling so sick, holding my stomach and talking to my pastor on the phone. He was there for me, just like our Lord and Saviour is there for us. It was always comforting to know that God was beside me as I went through such a rocky year.

Only a year later, my life has turned around. I have found that doing daily devotions is the only way to start my day, I don't do anything until my devotions are done. I will be the first one to acknowledge that if I miss my devotions, my day does not go well, I need that time in the morning to hear the Word of God and pray and talk to Him, to start my day.

Every day I ask for a little more direction and the courage to regain my life. I have been blessed by six wonderful friends who walk with me daily.

If you have never accepted Jesus as a personal Saviour, I would advise that you ask Him into your life today, then find a good church that will walk you through your Christian walk.

Colour Healing

Amber Houle

A few years ago, I was going through a very difficult time battling with depression, anxiety and post-traumatic stress disorder. I realized I needed to do something stress-free and creative that would make me happy to help the healing process along. As a first step I left my job. Bit by bit, I started painting and it definitely helped.

Dealing with my mental illness can be very hard, but I strive to do so. The more I expose myself to all the beauty that is in the world, the easier it is for me to not get stuck too long in the dumps.

BLEEDING HEALING HEART RECALL

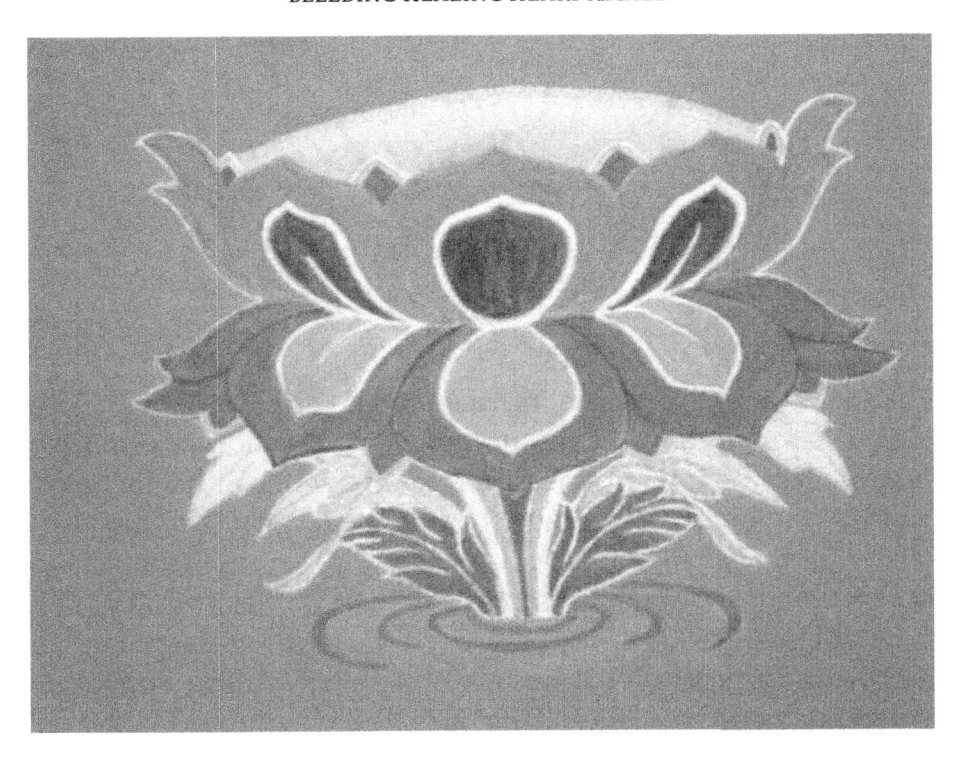

Continuing to Leap for Joy

Beth Bowman

Take a few deep breaths, relax, that's what they all tell me. Truth is that's a rough chore when you are in the metaphorical ditch. It's heavy, messy, slippery, smells and makes you want to lie down and let the muck to continue to slither over you. You may feel that your body keeps sliding back down as you reach out. There are two ways to look when finding oneself in the ditch. You can look at the muck and stay in it or you can reach out, Look Up and perhaps start to see a glimmer of light and catch a whiff of renewal, bit by bit.

Let me take you back to pre-ditch status. Life was really crazy but things were looking brighter. My eldest daughter had finally realized her dream for siblings in the form of twin sisters. Having experienced a still birth and a difficult end of a first trimester loss, I was grateful for the wee ones, who had just turned three. At the same time my body, mind and spirit was aching for a rest. I was off to visit my cousin on our annual late fall visit, though this time solo. My cousin and I were such close friends and our birthdays were days apart. Off we went to have a cherished adventure in the Mojave Desert to experience sleeping in a teepee and to run down sand dunes like little kids!

I leapt with joy in a beautiful Red Rock Canyon, outside Las Vegas, just the day before I hit the ditch. It's a special place I like to spend a day in during my stays.
It's breathtaking! My cousin insisted we take elegant and natural photos of me with such incredible landscape. A tribute and memory of my 40th birthday!

I'm grateful now that she thought of it, because within the following 24 hours we would find ourselves covered in sand and glass. Our belongings from the car were now scattered across a span of the Mojave Desert in California. There was no telephone service or buildings for miles from the accident. Luckily, we were found and aided by three hikers who thought they had witnessed an explosion and ventured to check it out.

There is the Beth 'before' the accident and the Beth 'after' the accident. Beth 'before' was an energetic, bubbly, lover of family and the patients she encountered through health care or hospice. Always on the go and fully booked, Beth 'before' didn't sit still very long. She was active. Beth 'before' thrived on gatherings with friends and their families as much as the schedule allowed. While not as active in the church as she once was, Beth 'before' liked to take the family to church and related functions when she had the chance to have a rare day off.

Beth 'after' the accident looked like a stooped over older lady. I wore a hat, scarf, sunglasses and a black winter coat the majority of the time. I wasn't able to tolerate light, loud noise and people who talked with their hands. I felt the need to cocoon myself for protection. Pain was constant and charged through my body and yet I was difficult to rouse. I drooled for a time and this lovely symptom still makes an appearance when I'm overtired, overstimulated and spent. There were many changes and adjustments. Who was this person that would ask repeatedly where the salt and pepper was during meals? I struggled to make sense of how long it would take to heal from this nightmare. Give me the medicine I need to take to cure this brain injury and quick. I felt I have enough to deal with my back, neck and soft tissue damage.

Pain charged my mind. It burned to look at a screen or bright light. My head hurt much of the time with my three young daughters who were eager to pray to God to heal their Mama. The charging weighed on with the realities of life, the state of my marriage, my lengthy recovery battle, the flashbacks and the nightmares from the accident itself. So much pain, in so many forms. How was I going to bear it? Did I want to? I admit it was doubtful numerous times. I had to figure out a way to get through this.

The Shift
The first realization was humility. It was going to take a community to get my family through this process. I had to admit I needed help, learn to ask for help and learn to be specific with my requests. This was hard. I'm the one who takes care of others. I had to really focus on how I was looking at and perceiving things. It required shifting my thoughts, a reframing to positive, when I got torn by the negative. Gratitude became everything. I had heard this all the time, but it is worth the effort.

I had to slow it down, give myself space to be mindful of my mind, body and spirit. What people and situations brought me the most comfort? It's definitely a process we need to continually refine, but it is more than possible to train your mind to show up for yourself. I had to learn to love this new version of myself. I had to know in my heart it was worth it!

The shift in thinking is a constant work in progress. The shift is not a single moment. It is millions of single moments we choose to be mindful and act in pure intent. That is the only thing we have the power to control: our response. The path to being mindful is far from perfect. Life throws us some curve balls or in my case rolls in the Mojave Desert, at high speed. It all comes down to a choice between two things. Are you going to do the recovery stuff just to get by or are you going to do this recovery work as the best version of yourself every day?

For me, this all came down to how did I want my three incredible daughters to overcome adversity and pain in their future? In my mind, that made it quite simple in the end. Note, I do not say it is easy. Beth 'before' would never foresee the challenges that threw her into the metaphorical ditch that day. Beth 'before' would never have imagined she had the skill, might and sheer determination to work away at coming out of that ditch.

My faith in God is what gave me the perseverance to get out of that ditch. Only He knew what wonderful plan was in store for my future. My faith, this trust in my higher power, was often tested. I came to learn that He picks you up when you least expect it and through earthly angels help comes in so many forms. He shows up when we think all else has failed and we think we are left behind. Faith carried me and continues to do so daily.

Every step we take forward is an example to those who are watching. That is faith in action! This is what I've found. The treasure here is that I like Beth 'after' so much more. She is a much better version of herself and refining daily. At the very heart of it was a saying I saw that often gave me the push; "She believed she could, so she did".

Jim Brown Our Unsung Sport Hero

Valentina Gal*

There seems to be no shortage of sports role models to look up to, nevertheless, when I met Jim Brown, a 66-year-young member of Spinal Chord Injury Ontario, I was most impressed with his accomplishments during the two summers 2011-2012. He may not have competed at the Paralympic Games, but he is definitely someone who we can all look up to.

Jim was interested in sports as a young person, being involved in running, gymnastics, football and scuba diving. He worked as a paramedic for 22 years. Since the equipment was not designed with ergonomics in mind, he sustained back injuries due to the stress of handling heavy equipment and several subsequent work accidents. He was diagnosed with paraplegia when he was 44. When I asked him how he dealt with the disappointment of not being able to walk and the depression that surely must have followed after discovering that he had paraplegia, Jim informed me that he had no time for those things. His wife Colette reminded him he had felt sad to have to replace his sports car with a specially equipped van. From his experiences and education at work, he knew what his future would be, so he made up his mind to take a different path. He committed himself to exercise and fitness.

Jim spent the next twenty years after his injury playing water sports like swimming and water volleyball. He also strengthened his muscles with weight training. During this time, he also advocated for people with disabilities by visiting schools and promoting equality and inclusiveness. Little did Jim know that his advocacy skills would come in handy on his own Pilgrim Journey.

In September 2010, Jim was diagnosed with seven blocked arteries due to conditions of heart disease and diabetes that he had in addition to paraplegia. The cardiologist did not want to do the heart surgery because he felt since Jim was in a wheelchair, he would not be able to sufficiently exercise after the operation.

"The Specialist couldn't believe it when I took off my suit jacket and tie and he saw that the muscles in my arms were twice the size of his," said Jim with a big smile. "I didn't stop living when I got my wheelchair." But Jim was not able to have his much-needed heart surgery without a fight. With the help of his doctors at Sunnybrook Hospital, in Toronto, he lost thirty pounds decreased the levels of his blood sugar and bargained to be part of a research group mixing vein with and without muscles to be used to repair the blockages in his heart. It took nine months before he was approved for surgery.

After the operation, Jim worked hard and didn't look back. He purchased a sea kayak and joined the Harbourfront Canoe and Kayak Centre in Toronto. He chose kayaking because it was a sport he could do and it was something that was visible on the water. From the first to the last day of summer, he put in eight hours a day with his hearing assistant dog Captain Daisy perched on her mat in the front of his kayak.

In 2011, his GPS unit indicated that he covered 1,200 kilometres and the next summer he more than doubled that distance to 2,600 kilometres. Jim kayaked in 22 different bodies of water, from Lake Simcoe to Lake Ontario, Erie and Huron, not to mention all the small lakes, canals and rivers he visited.

"You should see how people looked at me when they saw me being assisted out of my kayak into my wheelchair," said Jim. "They couldn't see that I had a disability when I was out on the water."

Along with the benefits of exercise, Jim's sport of kayaking allowed him to get back to nature. He renewed his passion for photography and said that he could get much more interesting pictures of the natural world by sneaking up on it from the water. "It's a totally different perspective." Jim once told me the kayak is much quieter than walking and can get into a lot of places that a powered boat can't go. Since the animals and the birds couldn't hear him coming, they were not afraid. He described an occasion when he sat in his sea kayak barely thirty feet away from a deer that was drinking at waters' edge. He saw the most wildlife in Toronto at the Toronto Islands.

"I wanted to have this story told," he said. "I almost did not have my heart surgery simply because I was labelled someone with a disability." He felt frustrated by how people treated him differently once they saw him get help into a wheelchair even though he kayaked farther than they had.

He continued to work towards the day when more people with disabilities in the community can stand up and take control of their own personal power. "I consider it more of an inconvenience than a disability." he said.

*Valentina Gal is a member of Spinal Cord Injury Ontario

Life Grief

Pauline Kiely – The Heart of a Horse
Scott Rose – Living in the Fog
Maria DeLuca – Fighting to Live
Denise Vernette – Loss of a Son – Art
Colette Cauli Brown – Termination Day Prediction
Dot Ernest – Life Altering Life
Colette Brown – Scottish Author – George Floyd

The Heart of a Horse

Pauline Kiely

It was late October, a moody day, windy and overcast. Over breakfast my husband casually mentioned, "There's a horse auction today, want to go?"

I replied, "Why not, we might find you a saddle." We had recently acquired two semi-retired twenty-something draft-cross trail horses named Monty and Argo. Horses being a relatively new venture for my new husband, but have been part of my life on and off since childhood.

In his late fifties this would be Michael's first livestock auction. I gave him the same advice that my father had given me, "Sit on your hands!" There was a lot of gear sold before the horses entered the ring, and we did manage to score a decent used western saddle. I had spent my time mulling over the tack not browsing the horses, but had noticed a lively chestnut that kicked out in the aisle. It was about the fifth horse to enter the ring, with a slight female passenger aboard. I whispered, "That's a young one."

Then the announcer proceeded to fill us in: "This 16.2 HH, three-year-old Trakehner mare has champion bloodlines. Unfortunately, this filly sustained a fetlock injury so is being offered today as a sound trail horse. The mare is up to date on vaccines, with sweet temperament."

I was impressed how the young mare showed no stress or fear in this animated setting. She appeared very noble, regal, and stopped dead in front of us completely fixated on my husband. The rider gave her a nudge, and she sauntered along, as the bidding crawled up to four hundred dollars. When this horse came around again, she put on the brakes on in front of Michael, who elbowed me, and I said, "No, two old people, two old horses!"

He said, "Honey, four hundred bucks is pretty cheap."

I said, "Honey, four hundred bucks is going to a meat guy." And I pointed to one man on the left, and another on the right, who I knew to be stock dealers.

Michael was horrified as the chestnut exited the ring. We hung around until the last whack of the anvil, paid for our saddle, and were on our way out when Michael paused to talk to the owner of this young Trakehner. She was visibly upset. He said, "I am sorry your horse didn't bring more money, she's very pretty."

And this woman swiped a tear and said, "I can't let her go for meat, but I can't take her home. My barn is full."

Michael asked, "What happened to her?"

"She was a high scoring premium foal full of potential that got caught in an electric fence at seven months. I poured a lot of money into the breeding, and the leg."

"How much did you want for her?" he asked.

"A thousand bucks, and a good home." she said.

I injected, "Doesn't anyone see a broodmare if anything else? I wouldn't breed her until she's at least six or seven though."

The owner smiled and said, "I like you already."

And Michael said, "If I give you twelve hundred will you deliver her?"

She said, "Really? Sure." And they sealed the deal with a handshake.

It was a bit of a backroom negotiation, but nobody had really bid on this horse except the meat guys, so in fairness, water finds its own level. Once we got into our car Michael said, "That horse needs us and I know I can fix her."

A few days later this filly arrived at our hobby farm. She wore a blanket which was promptly removed. I'd had horses for over forty years, and took the task of caring for them very seriously. This lanky chestnut was registered, her name was Hazeldeen. Everything they'd said was true with the exception of a sweet temperament.

Her coat was dull with a lot of dander. When I attempted to brush her she flinched, kicked, and nipped. It turned out to be rain-rot. I'd treated a horse for mange but this was something new to me. Hazel's left rear hoof was a weapon, her front left having sustained the injury. She was a bit toed-in, but otherwise sound. I knew I had my work cut out for me.

The old geldings had been friends for over ten years so there was no fanfare or welcoming committee for this sassy lass. Her eyes had so much expression, and she really flowed nicely, offering a natural extended trot on the lunge line but she couldn't be trusted. Over the course of those first twenty-four months Hazel constantly challenged me. She charged at me, cornered me, bit me, bit Michael, and kicked me twice.

I stormed into the house many times cursing her, declaring, "Take that unruly horse back to the auction. We have no idea how long she was caught in that fence, maybe there is brain damage? I am too old for this!"

I had two choices, give up or set some boundaries. So I dug in, watched videos, read Monty Roberts, *The Man Who Listens to Horses*, and Ariana Strozzi, *Horse Sense for the Leader Within*. It resonated, and I thought, "I got hit by a car, and nearly drowned as a child. I'd lost my father suddenly to an accident, been betrayed, and through a divorce. I know trauma."

My barefoot farrier, Mike Bogardis, came faithfully every six weeks. With his expert balanced corrective trims there was a noticeable improvement. It took a while, but at last Hazel let me saddle her up. When I got on her back, she planted her front feet and bucked about a dozen times and I was so beat up emotionally. Time for plan B. I'd win her over with kindness by having a carrot or treat in my pocket every time she saw me. I did this for about six weeks, and that one day I didn't have a bribe she lashed out at me again. "Okay," I said, "It's time for you and me to have a meeting of the minds. Horse, you do realize it is me or…nobody, nobody wants a bad horse! I am sorry that you got hurt, but I got hurt a time or two myself, and I didn't hurt you. You don't trust me, and I can't trust you. You have to stop being so bad and dangerous. I'm at my wits' end and tired of your nonsense."

I kept reading books, viewing more videos, and being good to her. With some quality hay, high mineral feed, and regular deworming, she matured to a healthy weight. With time and patience Hazel began to respond. After a couple of treatment baths, I could trust her to brush ninety percent of the time. Eventually she even let me ride her at a walk.

One day I wasn't paying attention while brushing her. My mind was brewing on some stress and drama. She swung her head around to nip me, but instead looked me in the eye. Intuitively I realized, "I am not respecting you as a sentient being. I am treating you like a chore on my list instead of enjoying and respecting our time together." I apologized, and the next time I came to see her I asked her to come to me, and she did. She brought her nose to my nose and we drew a few breaths together. Hazel began following me in the paddock, and focusing on me if I was outside. She whinnied for me in the morning, or when I arrived home. I was winning, or so I thought.

After almost three years of improved behaviours, out-of-the-blue, she lashed out at me again, and I was so disheartened. "Michael, I just can't trust her and that's no fun."

He, having a heart as big as himself, calmly said, "We've invested a lot of time and money in her, what are our options?"

I said, "I know an animal communicator, Lauren Bode. She is a psychic who can speak to horses."

"Call her."

When I spoke to my friend, she laughed, and said, "Pauline, your horse is crazy, she's crazy!"

I said, "Tell me something I don't know, that's why I'm calling you."

"Aw, she is showing me the accident. Everyone is upset, shouting, and barking orders. This is followed by needles and a series of operations. The people are disappointed because now she isn't perfect. They say she's worthless because she can't jump and do dressage. She can't show. Aw, the poor thing is so sad, everyone is so sad. She says she chose your husband because she knew he wouldn't let you give up on her. Pauline, you know how when you twist an ankle you tend to lean on the other side? This is what has happened. She has been compensating for the injury. You get an equine chiropractor in to realign her back, and you will have a new horse."

Holly at Horse and Hound recommended Kim Adie, who came out and spent over an hour on my sassy mare. The following day Hazel came out of the barn extending her back right leg, then her back left leg, farther than I've ever witnessed. It was a good big stretch as if to show me how sound she slept and how good she felt. About ten days later I began lightly riding my now six-year-old mare.

The following spring, we purchased a truck and trailer, and I joined the Ganaraska Forest Horse Club. After knee surgery Michael was unable to join us, but my grandson, Ayden, on his pony, Daisy, and Hazel and I thoroughly enjoyed the 9 km and up to 16 km trail rides. The camaraderie of this casual riding group was stellar and the trails just staggering.

Seabiscuit being my all-time favourite movie gets popped into the DVD player on occasion. Michael and I both tear up when trainer, Tom Smith, says, "You don't throw away a whole life just 'cause he's banged up a little."

Healing Hazel has helped me immensely. I've learned a lot about, and a great respect for, a horse's psyche. I am being educated in patience and tolerance, and reminded never to give up. There sure is some truth in the fact that she's a reflection of me. Almighty me who tended to take things for granted, generally in a hurry with a long to-do list. Today I savour and celebrate the big and little wins.

I read a poster recently that says, "The Horse is the wings a person feels inside." There certainly is truth in that.

Living in the Fog

Scott Rose

For the last ten years I have been living in the fog — when my mother took sick, my life stopped. I sold my house and moved back to the family home. Once there, I moved into my old bedroom and was Mom's 24-hour-a-day personal support worker until she passed away five years later.

The first year it was simple caring for her — cooking and cleaning and getting her to bed. On my free time I went for neighbourhood walks or caught a ballgame in the local park.

By year two, things got progressively worse. I only went out for a couple of hours at night and daytime walks and ballgames were a thing of the past. Mom received assistance from government-funded personal support workers and we hired some private ones as well. Every night, I slept with the lights on, never knowing if it was going to be the night that she would pass.

The week before she passed, I called 911 almost every day. I knew the end was drawing close. Mom passed in her sleep on a Sunday at 9:30 am.

After the emergency crews had left, I watched her body being taken down the road in a black van. My friends made plans for me to get away for a week to rest and relax. After that week away, I returned to my new reality. I had to deal with cleaning out her room, donating her clothes and getting rid of the medical equipment.

Then it hit me. There was no one around anymore. Not even a

phone call to break the silence.

My friends didn't call and the steady stream of support workers ended. I was alone. I had now walked into a very dense fog not knowing when I would see daylight again. This was the first sign that I had started grieving.

I was feeling like a pinprick on this big world. All my family was gone. After Mom passed away, my whole life went downhill. I stayed in the house for about a year before selling it to move to the country. I hoped country living would be more relaxing, but once there, I felt worse. With my closest neighbour a mile down the road, I felt so lonely. Still living in the fog and not knowing what I was to do with myself, I spent many days looking up to the heavens and asking why. I asked myself, what does life have in store for me?

I finally sold the country house and moved to a small community, where I knew more people. There are no photos of my parents on the walls which has seemed to create a cheerier house. I keep the drapes in the living room open. I find that particular spot so peaceful as there is a reflection on the glass that looks like three angels watching over me.

About five years have passed since my mother left to be with the Lord and I finally wake up full of life and energy — the sun beaming through the windows. My soul has been restored. My life has meaning.

I still have lots of mess to clean up but I no longer walk in the fog. I can see daylight again, knowing that Jesus accompanied me through the depths of my grieving. He never left me and sure did help along the way. Life is finally starting to return to the way it was ten years ago — before I put my life on hold to help my ailing mother. Every day is a new adventure and I am looking forward to enjoy those sun rays of life.

Life is Worth the Fight. Even at the Very End!

Marie DeLuca

When I was asked to submit something from the heart – what came to mind instantly was a poem by Dylan Thomas. For days I tried to come up with some other ideas but this poem, and it's meaning to me, would not leave me. So, I figured – this is what I am meant to share.

The following poem *"Do not go gentle into that good night"*, by author Dylan Thomas has a special meaning to me. It really is the basis of how I try to live my life. I guess the night I watched my dad leave this world, really brought this poem to light for me. My dad fought with every breath he took to Live. With every laboured breath, he exclaimed "NO". It was amazing and a true honour to have been with him that night.

I remember grabbing hold of my dad and telling him to relax, that we would all be ok. We would take care of mom, he could leave us in peace, and we would all be ok.

There is a line in the poem that captures the essence of the poem, my dad that December night, and my heart. I truly love this particular line – a line that holds such deep meaning to me.

Take a moment! Be courageous! Read the poem! Find that line. What meaning does it hold for you?

Although I believe Thomas's poem is talking about fighting old age - to me - it is all about fighting to **Live** and it reminds me of my dad, that December 30th, in the middle of the night, when he took his last breath.

Loss of a Son

Denise Vernette

This is what I have learned from life…you ask me to write something about how to deal with the loss of a child? Well, I can tell you that the day my son died I wanted to die too. I could not imagine my life without him, I just wanted to crawl in a hole and stay there.

Little by little, I started to do healing yoga and I realized that I was passing through life just going through the motions. I realized that the only thing that was truly mine was my life. I needed to be there for other people, accept what life was bringing me and be open to change.

Who said life is easy? We love, we get hurt by people and we go on. Meditation and working to accept whatever life brought me, helped me to realize that nothing lasts forever— nothing. We are just passing through this life.

We need to be open to love, accept people for who they are and always have an open heart.

I miss my son every day, but I know one day we will meet again. This is my earthly journey and I work to remain open to whatever life brings to me. I try to remind myself, when life serves you lemons try to make the best lemonade.

Through my art, I express my deep feelings of sadness, sorrow, healing and hope. My bench painting represents the emptiness I feel, while the birds represent peace.

My painting with a dove represents peace and love. We are all here on this earth to learn to live and love. The hardest part of life is to lose a loved one. It feels like the end of your world. I learned to live with this sadness. We all grieve differently. Like the old saying goes, time heals.

THE EMPTY BENCH

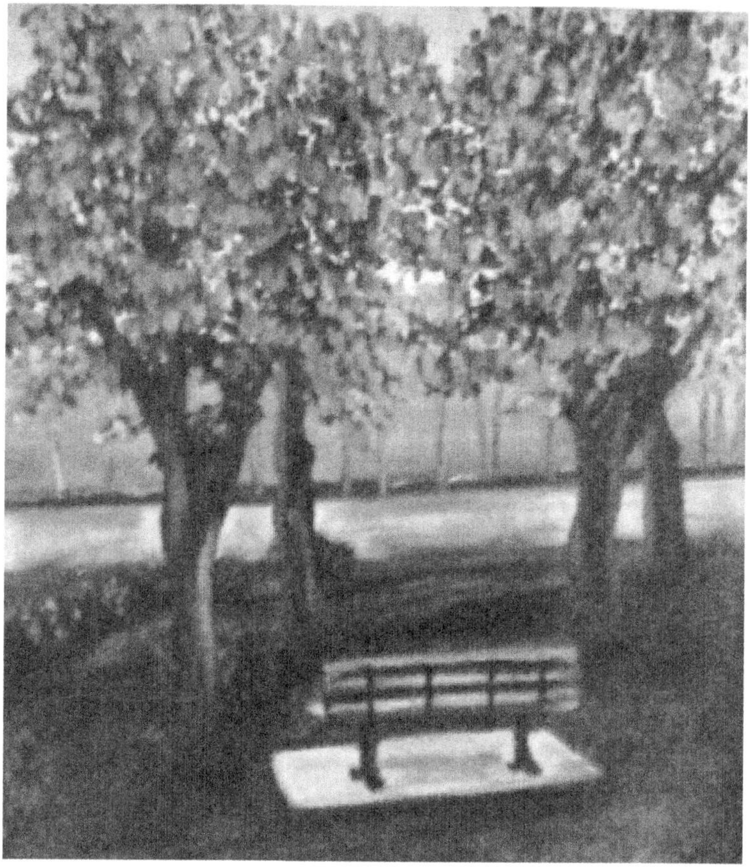

DOVE MEMORIAL

Termination Day Prediction

Colette Cauli Brown

Cousin Jessie shared a dream that Jim's mom Peggy (who had passed twelve years earlier) was coming to greet him with a suitcase and was getting ready to hug him, saying it would be the best Mother's Day ever – this year 2014. I was in shock. I remember talking to God and saying please if it is truly my Jim's time come and get him before or after Mother's Day because I did not want such a sad memory on my day. The Lord did hear me because Jim passed on May 8th, a few days before Mother's Day

My husband Jim told his family that "the cat with nine lives had reached his termination day." He prepared everyone for his passing to the Afterlife and said goodbye. I was there, our two sons, and their wives, our grandsons, and our granddaughter, and his two service dogs. Shep, the Golden Retriever had his head resting on Jim's left hand and Captain Daisy, his hearing alert dog, was at his left foot on the hospital bed looking at his master.

Jim told us he was heading to the Spirit World and a world without pain and he wanted us to focus on our lives, our path, our journey our Pilgrim Walk and he would be by our sides. Then he went into unconscious mode, very peaceful, and we could hear his breath in and out for seven hours.

At 10:00 a.m., he took his last breath. His canine companions knew right away. Shep followed Jim's Spirit out of the room and Captain Daisy turned her back to him and jumped off the bed. My sons and I did not realize it because we were anticipating another breath. My youngest son David said, "Mom do you think it was

Dad's last breath?" And so we all went closer, anticipating another breath. We were hoping beyond hope. Denying the reality… Then Ian, my eldest said, "The dogs knew. They left Dad's side because his Spirit is not there, and Shep followed his Spirit out the door."

My heart bled tears of lava. I lost my best friend, soulmate, my hubby, the father of our sons and the grandfather to our four grandchildren. I could not fall asleep on my bed and often slept sitting up on the leather sofa. My bedroom was redesigned. Still, I could not sleep in the room. After a move to a new house on the northern shores of Lake Scugog, I decided to buy something that would remind me of Jim. At a store that sells pillows, I saw one beige and brown with a stuffed dog on it and chose a special place in my living room to display it.

A few months passed. I was sad going through eye worries with a possible glaucoma diagnosis and was deeply afraid of losing my sight. Suddenly, the eyes of the stuffed dog on the pillow came to life. I checked the whole room for reflections, for lights, for TV flashes, wondering what caused the flashing eyes.

All of a sudden, complete peace of mind regarding my vision engulfed my whole body, heart and soul. I knew I would be all right, and I heard Jim's voice say that his worst worry was losing his hearing and mine was my sight! Jim managed quite well with his hearing assist companion, his service dog Captain Daisy. She was his guide while Jim kayaked on his Cardi-Yak Expedition and while Jim drove his car, alerting him to sirens and noises on road. At that moment in time, I felt Jim's presence right by my side as he had promised before he passed away to the Afterlife.

Life Altering Life

Dot Ernest

The death of a loving spouse or partner is different than other losses, in the sense that it literally changes every single thing in your world going forward. When your spouse dies, the way you eat changes. The way you watch TV changes. Your friend circle changes (or disappears entirely).

Your family dynamic/life changes (or disappears entirely). Your financial status changes. Your job, work or career changes especially if you were your spouse's caregiver before her or his passing.

Your self esteem is shaken, it affects your self-worth. Your confidence is affected.
Your rhythms are affected. The way you breathe, your mentality, your brain function is altered. (Ever heard the term 'widow brain?' If you don't know what that is, count yourself as very lucky.)

Your physical body deteriorates. Your hobbies and interests are at a standstill. Your sense of security is challenged. Your sense of humour is put on hold. Your sense of womanhood or manhood is affected.

EVERY, SINGLE, THING CHANGES! You are handed a new life that you never
asked for and that you don't particularly want. It is the hardest, most gut wrenching, horrific, life-altering impact that you have to live with.

The loss of your partner – after years of awakening only to find you are now alone – is sad. You feel your partner is still with you but there is no longer that physical contact nor the expression of simple words affirming love for each other.

The hurt and loss is less each year that passes and there is always hope to meet our spouse or partner in the future as we move on to a life after death.

Life altering life, a new Pilgrim Journey Ahead. One step forward at a time.

George Floyd

*Colette Brown**

I did not know you. You did not know me.
But I saw how you died, in the Land of the Free.
Gasping and moaning, scared and prone
You called for your mother, you begged for your life.
All of it captured on a by-passer's phone.
I cannot unsee it. I am witness to your strife.

Another black man murdered by a cop
By Trump and his cronies, the very white GOP.
But folk will say, no, it was just one bad officer.
If you are black, do you believe it, can you take that chance?
Or do you worry when your son leaves for work
Or your husband drives a delivery truck?

George Floyd, I did not know you, yet you are in my prayers,
A woman from Scotland, now more aware
Frightened for my friends in the US of A
As they look at their country and feel shame and dread.
The world holds its breath – will a dictatorship come
To the country of dreams and the Rule of Law?

George Floyd, I did not know you and you never knew me
But I cry tears of despair at what I cannot unsee.
I weep for your family, your friends, and their loss.
No more the lynching, the hunting, the burning cross!
You would not have died, would still have your breath
If your skin had been white when you walked on this earth.

George Floyd, I never knew you, but I will never forget.

While sharing the publisher's and contributing editor's name, this Colette Brown lives and writes in Scotland.

Rocking Chair Muse

Marg Nosworthy – Looking Back
Frederick H. Walker – The New You
Turtlette – Bleeding Warrior
Colette Cauli Brown – The Gift of Life
Sherry Crawford – Life Stages – Art
Nancy Robichaud- Longing

Looking Back

Margaret Nosworthy

In 1947, at sixteen years old, my parents told me it was time to go to the mill and get a job.

My two older brothers were continuing their education but there wasn't any value placed on my schooling. I remember sitting at my office desk thinking that I would marry, have ten kids and spend the rest of my life in the same small town.

Because I was a catcher for the marvellous pitcher on the mill's baseball team, I was asked to play fastball for a team that travelled from rural Guelph to play ball at Coxwell Stadium in Toronto, now known as Monarch Park Stadium.

The following year, miracles of miracles, I was asked to come to Toronto to play fastball in the only fastball stadium in the world for women. The first year I played left field with an intermediate team. The next summer, I played centre field with the intermediate team and travelled with the senior team when they played out of town.

In the off-seasons, I played basketball. In Toronto, I played using the men's rules for the first time in my life. There, I came to the attention of the coaches of a competitive women's basketball team. In the winter of 1948, the senior women's basketball team won the Canadian Championship. After some women moved on, I was asked to join the senior basketball team in the fall. We played against the high school boys' teams and much to their dismay, beat them every time.

The next summer, I again dug out my glove. Since I could play any position but pitcher, I was asked to travel with the senior team when they went to the United States to play. We also played at the Toronto Exhibition and once played an over-80 men's team from the USA.

After a few years of competitive baseball and basketball, I finally felt it was time to marry and have children. While I stopped competitive sports, I also got to have a rewarding career in the social community. I worked many years in housing at Warden Woods in Toronto.

Now, at age eighty-nine, I can look back and proudly say that I survived. People have been good to me along the way, helping me through my 'earthly healing journey'. I have had a wonderful life.

The New You

Fred H. Walker

The new you, is how my wife, Cathy, refers to me now, and I am sure she means it in a very positive way because I am not the man I was for most of my life. As far back as I can remember, until the sudden change, I was searching for purpose, to satisfy a void in my heart as to why I was alive. Careers were many, varying from Royal Canadian Mounted Police to United Church ministry, founding a non-profit organization to serve the Deaf Community, to setting up and running for thirty years a professional martial arts centre. To serve others was the hunger, but it was not filling that emptiness.

When a sudden experience brought me to a life-altering place, that did open my being to a realization of purpose and a path to follow. That realization and path could lead to very serious benefits for others brought to their knees, feeling like their heart was ripped from their chest and were in a very sad place.

In April of 2005, I was at an event in Kelowna, British Columbia. It was a weekend event that was almost over and we were having a social dance that Saturday evening before parting company. Well, I love to dance, especially to rock, the faster the better and that evening was no different. Great music and I am up doing my thing when I felt pain in my chest. Ignoring it I kept dancing. I was told by a doctor a way back that the pain was acid reflux from acid backing up, so I decided to keep dancing through it. Big mistake! I had a full cardiac arrest, dead before hitting the floor as told by one of the doctors who was there at the event. He and another doctor came to my aid trying to bring me back for 18 minutes. One hundred others apparently formed a circle and started calling me back in various spiritual ways depending on their faith, which I did obviously.

I was called the miracle man by the staff at the hospital as they didn't understand how I survived with no negative results.

The next day in the hospital I was so full of unconditional love it overflowed in the form of unstoppable tears. It was almost scary due to the fact that my character was very disciplined and intimidating for others.

After testing and finding my heart was indeed seriously blocked in two places and an operation was needed immediately, arrangements were made to do so while still out in B.C. An interesting thing was pointed out as they showed me the x-ray of my heart. In two places, my heart grew two arteries that crossed over to supply blood to blocked areas, which they were very surprised about. I was 60 years old at the time. It was clear that there was more to be done and it was not my time to go anywhere.

Now I am 76 years young and survived another open-heart surgery in 2014 and, as if this was not enough, when following up on recovery my doctor found a brain tumour. So, I was not long in having my head cut open and the tumour removed and yet, here I am still studying and learning at this point in my life? Well, it is based on the new me that Cathy refers to. My near-death experience revealed a truth to me that changed who I am and what needs to be done for the remainder of my time here.

One is, we do not die. No one dies. We simply change back to the energy we were before coming. Yes, crossing over is what we do and what is on the other side is unconditional love. There is NO EGO and all that comes from it.

Think about it. No egocentric thinking of any kind. How do we get to live this inconceivable life here? Sorry this cannot happen, but we can learn to get in touch with our soul that is within and learn how to connect to the same energy in other forms of life, plant, animal or people here as well as connect to the other side. We do have the capacity to love unconditionally here now. It is our purpose to learn how to quiet the ego and grow our love and compassion so the hunger to grow becomes motivation to look past the physical and reach out to areas intangible but with huge potential to change how we live.

Thoughts are energy and we manifest what we think so making the choice to have love your motive for all actions, mental, emotional, and physical, you will be A NEW YOU.

Bleeding Warrior Spirit

Turtlette – French/Algonquin Canadian

Spirit Walker's unconditional love of Norval Morrisseau's art legacy, spurred within him a Warrior Spirit, showcasing Norval's art, career, legacy and his Ojibway storytelling painted onto canvas.

Spirit Walker – also known as Ugo Matulic – responded to my request to know more about the artist after I won my bid on a Norval Morrisseau print. Deep in sorrow after the death of my hubby of 48 years, my best friend and soulmate, I was moved and brought back to life by the art of Norval Morrisseau, A fine quality print of his "Gathering of Shaman" was on display for a fundraiser in the local grocery store. Against all odds, my bid won and the print became mine. My spirit was touched to the core and uplifted allowing me to experience joy once again.

Spirit Walker dedicated years of impeccable research, documentation and selfless devotion to the memory of Norval Morrisseau, one of Canada's best-known artists, known as The Picasso of the North, and as a Shaman named Copper Thunderbird. Spirit Walker helped me through my healing journey to connect the meaning of Morrisseau's art to my life Pilgrim Journey.

Thank you from the heart, Spirit Walker. Many of Morrisseau's disciples have joined him in the Spirit World echoing their pride, support and passion to promote this great Ojibway Artist Norval Morrisseau for generations to come.

Spirit Walker, Ugo Matulic, a proud Croatian Canadian is the Guardian of Norval Morrisseau's Art and Culture's legacy to the World for future generations to cherish forever. Wishing to honour Spirit Walker's good friend Michael Moniz of Brampton,

Ontario, who departed to the spirit world far too soon in 2013, for his friendship and dedication to the memory of Norval Morrisseau since the blog's inception November 12, 2007. Bleeding tears flow down my cheeks as a French Algonquin Canadian, hoping that more Canadians will acknowledge and honour our Picasso of the North: Norval Morrisseau.

Albert Einstein believed our purpose is to find the reality of oneness instead as "something separate" from others. We may seem different but we are all interconnected trying to find purpose in this great, big, grand, tiny world of ours…Norval Morrisseau, by doing what he loved inspired, fortified and awakened the heart and spirit in others.

I so appreciate the overview of Norval Morrisseau's Earth Journey as so colourfully described in his quotes and his art. I admire his strong belief in his mission and purpose touching the inner spirit of all people who reside on Mother Earth for years to come.

Norval Morrisseau touched me to the core with his art piece "Gathering of Shaman."

"My art speaks and will continue to speak, transcending barriers of nationality, language and other forces that may be divisive, fortifying the greatness of the spirit that has always been the foundation of the Ojibway people. My people believe the earth to be their mother and that we are children of the earth. In spirit we are one with our environment. We are all one in Spirit."

Norval Morrisseau- Copper Thunderbird
March 14th, 1931 – December 4th, 2007

ᓂᒪᓯᓂᐱᐦᐃᑫᐃᐧᐣ ᐊᔭᒥᐦᐃᐍᒪᑲᐣ ᒥᓇ ᑲᐯ ᑕᐱᒥᐊᔭᒥᐦᐃᐍᒪᑲᐣ, ᒋᐱᒥᑕᐃᐧᓂᑫᒪᑲᑭᐣ ᑲᑭᐱᐡᑲᑯᐘᐨ ᐊᓂᔑᓂᓂᐘᐠ, ᐃᔑᑭᒉᐃᐧᓂᐠ ᒥᓇ ᑯᑕᑭᔭᐣ ᑲᐡᑭᐦᐅᐃᐧᓇᐣ ᑫᑭᐅᒋ ᒪᒋᓂᐡᑭᑫᒪᑲᑭᐣ, ᒋᒪᐡᑲᐃᐧᓯᐡᑲᑫᒪᑲᐠ ᐊᒐᑯᐃᐧᓂᐠ ᑲᐯᐦᐃ ᑲᑭᐅᒋᐱᒍᓂᑯᐘᐨ ᐅᒋᐍ ᐊᓂᔑᓂᓂᐘᐠ.

ᓂᑕᓂᔑᓂᓂᒪᐠ ᐅᑌᐍᑕᓇᐘ ᐊᐦᑭᓂ ᐁᐅᒪᒪᒥᐘᐨ ᒥᓇ ᐁᐅᓂᒐᓂᓯᒥᑯᔭᐠ **ᐊᐦᑭ. ᐊᒐᑯᐃᐧᓂᐠ** ᑭᐯᔑᑯᒥᐣ ᐃᒪ ᒥᓯᐍ ᑲᐊᐱᒐᐠ ᑭᑕᑭᒥᓇᐣ.

ᑭᐯᔑᑯᒥᐣ ᐊᒐᑯᐃᐧᓂᐠ.

ᓇᐧ*> ᒪᐧ*ᓯ
ᒥᐢᑲᐧᐱᐠ ᐊᓂᒥᑭ
(ᐊᓂᔑᓇᐯ)
ᒥᑭᓯᐃᐧᐱᓯᑦ 14, 1931 - ᒪᑯᒉᑭᔑᑲᐣᐱᓯᑦ 4, 2007.

Norval Morrisseau's quote translated by Elvire Mekoudjou, Win-translation
Oji-Cree Dialect in the artist's honour.

The Gift of Life

Colette Cauli Brown

"How brave to enter a body and dance the dance of existence only to lose everything imagined to be true in the moment of death."

Annie Kogan

A mother-in-law is sometimes addressed as "mother." Often, it is followed by the last name, like Mother Smith. I had a special bond with, and special name for, my adoptive mother-in-law: Mother Mary. She survived the loss of two loving husbands, and three of her four children. She heroically faced tragedy and served as my inspiration.

Now Mother Mary truly knew the lives she touched and the victories she accomplished in her 102 years of life on earth. She showed her inner glow to the people in her life: babes, youth, teens and grownups alike. Whatever your faith, beliefs, abilities. Whatever your sexual orientation, family history or choices in life! Never judging, always giving her love and understanding to everyone who crossed her path.

And last year, when at death's door, I remember her asking me "Why am I still here in my room?" My answer: "Look around you at all the lives you are still touching in your room at Fairview in Cambridge, Ontario. And every person you encounter, every challenge you face, has been part of your journey!"

In 1958, Mother Mary rescued a next-door neighbour in St. Jacob and best friend to her youngest son Rae, my James, who became an orphan at age 12. She gave James his first bible and talked to him about the original Mother Mary. She was aware of the sorrow of this young orphan and shared with him how sad Mary the mother of Jesus was on Christmas Day.

Mother Mary and Lorne Shantz, her second hubby, drove to Timmins to stand up as parents for this orphan. Being Mennonite, they received communion with the blessings of Father Cascien in a Roman Catholic Church. And on that day September 16, 1967, at my wedding to James, Mother Mary became my psychological mom too. Eventually, Grandma to our two sons: Ian and David and great-grandma to our four grandchildren: Dalton, Ethan, Darby and Garrett. She introduced our family to the game of Crokinole which is still a game of choice for all of us. Our sons played with Mother Mary's vintage marble game with a creative wooden design. We enjoyed choir recitals, live mangers at Christmas and meals at Harmony Lunch, a favourite family hangout in Kitchener-Waterloo.

Mother Mary played pool at Fairview with our grandchildren. And she explored the iPad with our granddaughter. Always open, loving, caring, humble, soft spoken and chatty.

Mother Mary accepted unconditionally all forms of visible and invisible disabilities. My idol, my role model! My inspiration! Mother Mary's parting gift to everyone: "Family, friends, live, love, laugh, hope and pray. Be a loving smile to everyone you meet on your earthly journey!"

I remember her son Rae once chastising his mom for not taking care of a dead plant up on the shelf near her window, while all the other plants and flowers flourished with her loving care. Mother Mary's response: "I'm saving that one bulb for a friend to plant in her garden..." She even saved dead plants to be reborn again from her room at Fairview. Mother Mary admired the uniqueness of every leaf, snowflake, every sunset, every star in the Heavens.

I remember her favourite poem: One Little Rose (author unknown)

I would rather have a rose,
From the garden of a friend,
Than flowers strewn around my casket
When my days on earth must end!

I would always bring her a rose from my garden to honour Mother Mary.

Life's Stages

Sherry Crawford

Sherry is an Algonquin Artist residing in the Peterborough area, and a proud member of the Kijicho Manitou Madaouskarini Algonquin Nation, Bancroft, Ontario, Canada. She has been **picking up the pieces** of her stolen Culture for over 25 years and is grateful for the Spiritual Teachings that she has been able to acquire through Ceremony and Elders. She believes it is important to share these teachings through her **ART! She describes this particular art piece called LIFE STAGES.**

The painting below named LIFE'S STAGES has come through in stages. Just like our lives! The connections between every human and all things are represented in the black lines. The upper world, middle physical world, and the lower world — this painting shows we are continual flow.

WE are energy. We refer to the trees as 'Standing People' because they are our brothers and sisters, supplying us with much needed clean air! The 'standing person' on the left...facing east, represents the **Contemplation stage of life** where we plan out our experiences, the white dots represent the people we have chosen to share our next lifetime with.

The next tree, represents our **Birth**. The white dots represent the people who are in our circle at your time of birth. The next represents **Life** and the people who bring us our life experiences. The last, represents our **Death,** and the people who will mourn and keep us connected through their hearts and love. The white hole at the bottom right, is a **'portal to the astral'** which we can find in nature and meditation.

All of the answers we seek are there! Let us not forget, we choose these lifetimes willingly. The Mysterious Circle of Life... If we hurt one another, we hurt ourselves! Right now, I'm grateful to be in the **'living'** stage!

Miigwetch for reading!

Longing

Nancy Robichaud

The birds are gathering,
Flying, soaring,
As we used to do.

Enjoying the air,
Seemingly without care,
As we used to do.

Waiting for Spring
To have their young
All will be new

Buds on the trees,
Green fresh grass
As it used to be.

Maybe we too will
Someday be set free…
The way we used to be?

About The Author

Colette Cauli Brown

Colette Cauli Brown known as Coletta, Turtlette, Colette Fortier, Cauliflower, Gamma, Crazy Grandma and Nana Bear is a retired clinical social worker. With more than thirty-five years in the field, Brown has witnessed the healing journey of many and invited individuals to celebrate their Pilgrim Journey in a collection of their stories at various stages of their lives.

Bleeding Healing Heart Recall is the result of that invitation and Brown is proud of her role in publishing the book and serving as contributing editor.

She is a passionate environmentalist with an ongoing mission to rescue turtles. Brown enjoys teaching children, youth and adults the art of creative expression; helping them create poems, songs, stories, skits, journals and draw their feelings through expressive art.

Brown promotes Abilities In Motion (https://www.abilitiesinmotion.ca/) – inclusive accessible paddling for everyone. She is also a volunteer at WindReach Farm (http://windreachfarm.org/) in Ashburn, Ontario. She enjoys kayaking, canoeing, dragon boat paddling, horseback riding. She is an avid photographer sharing her photos on viewbug.com called cardiyakexpeditionajbrown - Colette Brown. She is a Pilgrim walker and enjoys travelling.

Author Colette Cauli Brown lives and writes in Whitby, Ontario,

Canada.

Her previous five books are available:

Ebooks:
htttps://www.smashwords.com/profile/view/turtlette

Print:
http://www.palimpsestpress.ca/index.php

Acknowledgement

I am grateful to the many friends and professionals who shared their ideas, expertise and valuable time, and were willing to share their grief recall and contributed to assist me in publishing this book: Bleeding, Healing Heart Recall. In particular, I would like to thank the following people:

Pauline Kiely a freelance writer and author for her contribution, her spirit and encouragement through this process.

Ruth E. Walker of Writescape for her editing expertise and support.

Visual artist Cathy Walker of Cathy's Covers, for designing the cover and layout.

Michael Bryant for his guidance and referral to a printer.

The following women, for their support and contributions.
Rachel Weeda, Madeleine Boznar and Lina Crawford: birth sisters; Fran Grant, Dorothe McKinlay, Jane Walker, Marg Nosworthy, Eve Hunter, Arianna, Pat Van Der Veen, Tami DeJong, Marci Anderson, Nancy Robichaud, Beth Bowman, Sherry Crawford, Colette Brown, Denise Vernette, Amber Houle, Lisa Petkovich, Maria Deluca, Silvia de Abreu, Dorette Chen, Linda L. Kriner, Pauline Halstead, Alivia Lusk, Emma Lusk, Abby Lusk, Grace Curnock, Janice Higgins, Chelsea Mack, Llyn Loveday Clark: spirit sisters for their love and support.

Dot Ernest, Ernest Scullion, William Morgan, Scott Rose and Frederick H. Walker for their support and contributions to my book.

My Healing Heart Bible study group at Brooklin Village Church for sharing and supporting one another during our healing journey.

My pilgrimage group, at Brooklin Village Church and led by Uriah Pond, for helping me focus on my pilgrim life journey ahead.

Lisa, Ian, Tina, David, Dalton, Ethan, Darby, Garrett: the Brown clan – Barry & Margo Hartford and Claude & Gail Mathe - the sparkles in author's life that shine and illuminate her heart and spirit.

Shep and Daisy: canine guardians – earth angels guiding my path.

Colette Cauli Brown,
known as Turtlette, Coletta, Colette Fortier and Nana Bear

Made in the USA
Monee, IL
07 June 2021